BRAVE
VOLODYMYR

The Story of **Volodymyr Zelensky** and the Fight for **Ukraine**

Written by **Linda Elovitz Marshall**

Illustrated by **Grasya Oliyko**

Quill Tree Books

An Imprint of HarperCollinsPublishers

Volodymyr Zelensky was born in Ukraine, a country with a beautiful flag. The top half of that flag is clear blue, like the Ukrainian sky. The bottom half is bright yellow, like the Ukrainian fields of wheat and corn, sunflowers and barley.

Ukrainians are very proud of their flag.

But when Volodymyr was a child, no one was allowed to fly it. In those days, the Soviet Union ruled Ukraine, and flying Ukraine's flag was against the law.

The Soviet Union was a group of countries that included Ukraine. Laws were made in its capital, Moscow, which was located in Russia.

The Soviet Union made laws for everything:

where people could work,

what people could say,

and what people could call their country.

Ukraine was called the Ukrainian Soviet Socialist Republic.

Anyone who broke the rules or said the wrong thing or criticized the Soviet government could be punished.

For example, when the Soviet government lied and said a famine that starved millions of Ukrainians never happened, no one was allowed to disagree.

Volodymyr, like many others, knew about those lies.

And Volodymyr hated lies.

Volodymyr was an only child. He lived with his parents in Kryvyi Rih, a large industrial city. His father was a professor. His mother, an engineer.

The Zelensky family was Jewish. For more than a thousand years, Jewish people have lived in Ukraine.

Ukraine, however, wasn't always kind to the Jewish people. Throughout the country's history, Jews were often discriminated against and bullied . . . or worse.

Volodymyr's family—like millions of Jewish people—suffered under the Nazis during World War II. Several of his family members perished.

As a soldier in the Soviet Army, Volodymyr's grandfather fought against the Nazis during World War II. The Soviet, American, and other European allied forces defeated the Nazis.

Then, in 1991, when Volodymyr was almost thirteen years old,
something unbelievable,
    impossible to imagine,
        and very important took place. . . .
            The Soviet Union fell apart!
Countries that had been part of the Soviet Union
became independent. And that meant Ukraine was free!
Now Ukrainians could make their *own* laws
and fly their *own* flag.

Volodymyr was so happy. It was a new start for all Ukrainians.
With this new freedom came so many possibilities!
But freedom is a fragile thing.
It needs to be cherished.
It needs to be protected.
And freedom depends on truth.

Volodymyr knew his country's problems, its history, its sorrows. He wanted to help make Ukraine a better, kinder, more joyful place.

Volodymyr spoke Russian and Ukrainian. He learned English, too. He attended university in his home city. He studied law and planned to become a lawyer. And at the university, he became good friends with his future wife, Olena, who was studying architecture.

Volodymyr joined a comedy team and competed in a show called *KVN* (*Club of the Funny and Inventive*), and they won.

They were on TV again and again. Being funny was ... fun!

But could he make the world a better, kinder, more joyful place by being funny?

He could try.

So, instead of practicing law, Volodymyr started an entertainment and production studio. He called it Studio Kvartal 95.

Volodymyr acted.

He danced with the stars.

He made funny faces

and spoke in silly voices.

He even became the Ukrainian voice of **PADDINGTON BEAR**.
What fun!
What joy!
What freedom!

While Volodymyr was making people laugh at work and cuddling his first child at home, Ukraine held its 2004 presidential election.

Volodymyr—and the whole country—eagerly awaited the election results.

What would happen?

Who would lead Ukraine on its road to freedom?

But when the election results came out, they were filled with lies.
Not all the votes were counted. The election was not fair, and the
candidate chosen by Russia's President Vladimir Putin won.

Ukrainians protested. They marched for freedom, for honest
elections. Their voices were heard.

Another election—a fair one—was held.

This time, Viktor Yushchenko was elected president.

There was hope for Ukraine.

Over the next few years, Ukraine grew and changed.

Another election was held. President Viktor Yanukovych replaced President Viktor Yushchenko.

Volodymyr and Olena's family grew and changed, too.

They had a second child.

Ukrainians enjoyed their independence.

But to be *really* independent from Russia, Ukrainians wanted something more: membership in the EU—the European Union.

With EU membership, Ukrainians could live the way people in free European countries lived.

President Viktor Yanukovych promised that Ukraine would join the EU.

He prepared to sign the membership papers.

Everyone was so excited, especially Volodymyr.

At last, Ukraine would really be independent.

But just before the papers were signed, President Yanukovych of Ukraine met with President Putin of Russia and . . .

President Yanukovych broke his promise.

He refused to sign the papers.

Twenty-three years after Ukraine's independence, Russia's government was still trying to control Ukraine.

All over the country, Ukrainians—including Volodymyr—were angry.

Thousands of Ukrainian citizens—young and old—protested for months.
They signed petitions.
They marched and sang.
They even slept in a city park in the center of Kyiv,
the capital of Ukraine.

But how did President Yanukovych of Ukraine respond?
He deserted his country. He fled to Russia.

Things got worse.

Russia took control of the Crimean peninsula in the southern part of Ukraine.

But no one in Crimea was allowed to protest because with Russia in control of Crimea, protesting was against the law—just like when Russia controlled the rest of Ukraine. Ukrainians were angry and sad and worried.

But what could they do?

What could ANYONE do?

Then Volodymyr Zelensky—the actor, dancer, movie star—
had an idea.

An exciting idea.

A brilliant, creative, sparkling **IDEA**!

What if he used humor and truth to make his country a better
place—to *show* people the lies they were being told,
to *show* what was wrong with their country
and with what was happening?

Working with Olena and his production studio, Volodymyr created a television series called *Servant of the People.*

It was about an exceptionally honest high school teacher who hated lies, who pointed out what was dishonest and corrupt in his country.

Then, in the show, that high school teacher ran for president . . . and **WON**.

The star of the show was . . . **VOLODYMYR ZELENSKY**.

The series portrayed Ukraine's successes. It also showed Ukraine's problems.

Volodymyr produced it with humor and with heart . . . and with hopes of making Ukraine a better place, a kinder place.

But some things—like keeping a country free, honest, and independent—could not be fixed with humor.

So Volodymyr Zelensky—actor, dancer, star—ran for president *for real* . . .

because he knew that freedom is a fragile thing.

It needs to be cherished.

It needs to be protected.

And freedom depends on truth.

Volodymyr Zelensky won the 2019 election by a landslide.

He became President Zelensky.

But President Putin of Russia wanted to control more and more of Ukraine.

In February 2022, he sent troops into Ukraine to encircle and destroy its cities, towns, and villages—large and small.

He even tried to capture Kyiv, where President Zelensky lived and worked.

The Ukrainians were strong even though the huge Russian army outnumbered their forces.

It was like David fighting the giant, Goliath.

What was President Zelensky to do? He needed help.

The United States offered to fly him and his family somewhere safe.

But brave Volodymyr said no. "The fight is here," he said. "I need ammunition, not a ride."

He stayed in Ukraine to protect his country and his people.

On television and radio, through the internet and on social media, brave Volodymyr showed the world what was happening.

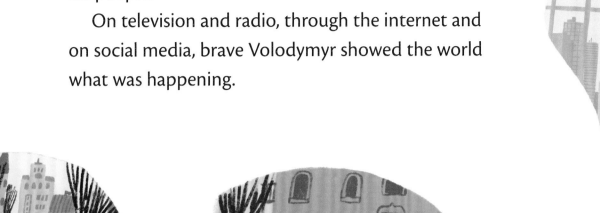

He said his country was a peaceful country.

It did not want war.

But "if we face an attempt to take away our country, our freedom, our lives and the lives of our children, we will defend ourselves."

And the Ukrainian people did just that.

President Zelensky said that a threat to Ukraine is a threat to all.

He said that to save Ukraine and to defend freedom everywhere, everyone must act together to resist the Russian army and oppose President Putin's war against Ukraine.

President Zelensky did not blame the Russian people, who faced arrest if they protested.

Help poured into Ukraine.

From around the world, doctors, nurses, volunteers, soldiers, and teachers came.

Countries and businesses—everyone who could— sent food, medicine, and supplies.

All over the world, people waved Ukraine's blue-and-yellow flag,
baked blue-and-yellow cookies,
painted blue-and-yellow signs,
sent money,
planted sunflowers,
and opened their homes to Ukrainian refugees.

People helped in every way possible.

President Volodymyr Zelensky
led the courageous Ukrainian people
in the fight against the giant Russian army.
And day after day, brave President
Volodymyr Zelensky reminded
the world that an attack
on one is an attack on all—
that freedom is a fragile thing.
It needs to be cherished.
It needs to be protected.

And freedom depends on truth.

AUTHOR'S NOTE

My great-grandparents came to the United States from what is now Ukraine. They lived in Zolochiv, in the area called the Pale of Settlement.[1] Back then, that was the *only* area where most Jews were allowed to live. Jews could *visit* other places for commerce or entertainment, but they could *settle* only in the Pale.

At times, the Pale was ruled by the Russian Empire. Other times, it was ruled by Poland or Austria or Ukraine. So, my great-grandparents came from Ukraine or Poland or Austria or Russia. It depended on the year.

But no matter which country ruled, some things stayed the same—repression and anti-Semitism (the hatred of Jews). When my great-grandparents were able to, they left for the United States—for freedom and for a better life.

One summer, I participated in a project that brought together youth from around the world to work for peace. Participants came from many countries: Czechoslovakia (now Czechia and Slovakia), Romania, Italy, Sweden, Algeria, the Netherlands, and the United States (like me). Our project, in Lesná, near the industrial city of Chomutov in what is now Czechia, was to restore a waterway that was destroyed during World War II. Speaking many languages, we worked as a group toward the same goal.

That project took place in 1969, exactly a year after the Czech people attempted to gain their freedom from the Soviet Union. Their 1968 attempt was crushed by the Russian government. Russian tanks rolled in. People were arrested and taken away. Yet the spirit of their movement and the spirit of freedom lived on.

In 1969, I stood with friends from my work project in the place where Russian tanks had crushed the rebellion the previous year. My friends and I were in a crowd of thousands. Once again, Russian tanks barged through the streets. Soldiers, speaking through bullhorns, called from the tanks: Leave. Now. Disperse.

One friend, a medical student from Italy, took photos. He was arrested immediately and taken away. Terrified, many of my friends fled to their home countries. I called a Czech friend who lived in Prague. He took me to his mother's home, where they fed and sheltered me until it seemed safe to leave. Then they escorted me to the train station. I took a train to Vienna, Austria, where I knew no one but where we knew I would be safe.

Now Ukraine, once home to my family, is being assaulted by President Putin and his Russian troops. Now it is as if I am once again standing in the path of tanks. But now Ukraine has a Jewish president, whose family perhaps lived not far from my family.

My heart is there, in Ukraine.

Unless we stop the horrors, they will continue . . . in country after country. . . . No place will be safe.

This book is my way of speaking out, of coming to the defense of the people in Ukraine.

Because freedom is a fragile thing.

---

1. Pale of Settlement—this unusual phrase derives from the Latin word *palus*, meaning "stake." It was, literally, a staked-out territory in which Jewish people were allowed to settle.

TIMELINE

January 25, 1978—Volodymyr Zelensky is born to Rymma Zelenska and Oleksandr Zelensky in Kryvyi Rih, an industrial city in southern Ukraine where iron is mined. As a small child, Volodymyr and his family live in Mongolia for his father's work. When he returns to Kryvyi Rih, he begins school.

August 24, 1991—Ukraine declares independence from the Soviet Union.

December 25, 1991—The Union of Soviet Socialist Republics (the Soviet Union) comes to an end and Soviet Union President Mikhail Gorbachev resigns. Power is transferred to the new president of the Russian Federation (Russia), Boris Yeltsin.

1995—After declining an opportunity to study in Israel, Volodymyr begins studies at the Kryvyi Rih Economic Institute (part of Kyiv National Economic University). Volodymyr performs in a comedy group called Kvartal 95 (named for the quarter, or neighborhood, where he grew up).

1997—Volodymyr and Kvartal 95 compete in a comedy competition on a TV show called *KVN* (*Club of the Funny and Inventive*). They win.

1997–2003—Volodymyr and Kvartal 95 return regularly to perform on television.

2000—Volodymyr graduates with a law degree.

September 6, 2003—Volodymyr and Olena marry.

2003—Volodymyr cofounds an entertainment studio and production company called Studio Kvartal 95. He is the artistic director.

July 15, 2004—Volodymyr and Olena's first child, a daughter named Oleksandra, is born.

November 2004–January 2005—Following the run-off vote of the 2004 Ukrainian presidential election, a series of protests against corruption, voter intimidation, and electoral fraud erupts. The protests, named for the orange political campaign colors, are called the Orange Revolution.

2011—Volodymyr becomes general producer of Inter TV, a Ukrainian television channel.

2012—Volodymyr begins his film career, acting in movies.

2013—Volodymyr returns to Kvartal 95 as artistic director.

January 21, 2013—Volodymyr and Olena's second child, a son named Kyrylo, is born.

November 2013—President Viktor Yanukovych meets with President Vladimir Putin. Following that meeting, President Yanukovych refuses to sign a promised agreement for Ukraine's entry into the European Union (EU). Protests erupt.

February 2014—After months of protests, Yanukovych flees to Russia. The Ukrainian parliament installs a temporary government.

March 2014—Crimea, which is part of Ukraine and has an important seaport on the Black Sea, is claimed (annexed) by Russia. On March 18, President Putin formally declares Crimea part of Russia.

May 2014—Billionaire Petro Poroshenko is elected president of Ukraine.

November 2015–March 2019—Volodymyr stars in his television series *Servant of the People*. In it, he plays a high school teacher. Disgusted with government lies and corruption, the TV teacher runs for president . . . and wins.

April 2019—Volodymyr is elected president of Ukraine.

2021—In a series of military buildups, tens of thousands of Russian soldiers assemble at the border with Ukraine.

February 24, 2022—Russian invasion of Ukraine begins. Russia's President Putin calls the invasion a "special military operation." Russians are forbidden to use the word "war" or to be critical of the war in any way. Doing so can result in fines and long prison sentences. Millions of Ukrainian women and children flee their country. Millions more move into other parts of Ukraine as civilian infrastructure is destroyed.

BIBLIOGRAPHY

Bahr, Bob. "Zelenskyy Emerges as Jewish Hero in Ukraine," *Atlanta Jewish Times*, March 7, 2022, https://www.atlantajewishtimes .com/zelenskyy-emerges-as-jewish-hero-in-ukraine/.

Cramer, Philissa. "18 things to know about Volodymyr Zelensky, showman, 'Paddington' voice and Jewish defender of Ukrainian democracy," *Jewish Telegraphic Agency*, March 1, 2022, https://www.jta.org/2022/03/01/global/18-things-to-know-about -volodymyr-zelensky-showman-paddington-voice-and-jewish-defender-of-ukrainian-democracy.

Ray, Michael. "Volodymyr Zelensky." In *Encyclopedia Britannica Online*, Encyclopedia Britannica, Inc., 2022. Article published September 27, 2019; last modified March 22, 2023. https://www.britannica.com/biography/Volodymyr-Zelensky.

Terkel, Amanda. "After Claiming He Wanted to 'Denazify' Ukraine, Putin Strikes Holocaust Memorial Site," *HuffPost*, March 1, 2022, https://www.huffpost.com/entry/vladimir-putin-babyn-yar-ukraine_n_621e6b83e4b0783a8f075d6b.

Zelenskyy, Volodymyr. "The future of the continent is being decided by us with our resistance and by our friends with their help." Speech, Office of the President of Ukraine, Kyiv, Ukraine, March 7, 2022, https://www.president.gov.ua/en/news/majbutnye -kontinentu-virishuyemo-mi-svoyim-sprotivom-i-nashi-73397.

ACKNOWLEDGMENTS

Invaluable and much-appreciated assistance for which the author is deeply indebted and
thankful came from Toby Trister Gati. Mrs. Gati was Special Assistant to President Bill Clinton
for Russia, Ukraine, and the Eurasian States at the National Security Council and worked in the
U.S. State Department for several years. She is a member of the Council on Foreign Relations.

To Gabriel, Niomi, Julia, Lyra, Avigail, Talia, Leah, Noa, Baruch, Ezra,
Aviya, Orly, Ellie, David, Sarai; to the Gati children and grandchildren;
and to brave Volodymyr Zelensky and all the children of Ukraine
—L. E. M.

To the brave Ukrainian people
—G. O.